THE UNAUTHORIZED BIOGRAPHY

SCOOP!

ISSUE #4

The Jonas Brothers

by Jennifer Poux

Grosset & Dunlap

GROSSET & DUNLAP
An Imprint of Penguin Random House LLC, New York

Illustrations by Becky James

Photo credit: cover: Jesse Grant/Stringer/Getty Images Entertainment/
Getty Images North America

Visit us online at www.penguinrandomhouse.com.

ISBN 9780593222287   10 9 8 7 6 5 4 3 2 1

TABLE OF CONTENTS

• •

CHAPTER 1

THAT'S THE WAY THEY ROLL

*N*ick, Kevin, and Joe: They're super talented, objectively hot, world famous, and married to absolute queens. And now . . . the Jonas Brothers are back!

If you're Gen X or older Gen Z, you're thinking: finally! If you're on the younger side of Gen Z, you wouldn't remember the first iteration of the world's favorite band of brothers. But if you're a new stan, fan, or just Jonas-curious, you are here for the Jonas renaissance! Or, the *Jonaissance*, as we like to call it here at SCOOP! Either way, that makes for a lot of cross-generational fans buying their music and lining up to see them live. So it's a no-brainer their comeback game is *100 percent*.

Maybe you've been in love with Nick forever.

Maybe you just discovered Joe. Maybe you think Kevin has morphed into the cutest bro. (Sorry, they're all taken.) Or maybe you want to be one of them. (Who could blame you?) The JoBros are about as close to pop royalty as you get. And they're way less controversial than many of their predecessors (see: Michael Jackson and Madonna).

Whatever your interest in this sibling trio, there's so much to know about the Jonases, from their earliest days as Jersey kids to their savage resurgence on stage, TV, and film. Their bios are long, their credentials run deep, their love lives are the stuff of rom-coms. But it all began in a little, unassuming brick house in suburban Wyckoff, New Jersey, where music was king. That is, right after religion.

That's right! The Jonas Brothers began as a family band with religious roots. Dad was a pastor, and after preaching in Arizona and Texas, the family returned to New Jersey and settled in for a while. The Jonas family—parents Kevin Sr. and Denise, kids Kevin Jr., Joe, and Nick (Frankie Jonas wasn't in the mix yet)—lived in the parsonage down the street from the Wyckoff Assembly of God church, their second home. Nick says they were basically the first family of the church, which came with perks and pressures. (More on that later!)

Music was a major focus at home, where Kevin Sr. played a number of instruments and both parents liked to sing. Clearly, the Jonas Brothers have music in their DNA. It was also a focus of the church, where the boys were immersed in music and performance, especially Nick. Early on, Kevin Sr. says he knew Nick had a gift. When Nick was just three, he would self-correct if he sang a bad note! Whoa! But it was in a hair salon (Denise was in the chair) when Nick was six that another customer noticed his angelic voice and recommended a talent manager to his mom. At eight, he started acting in Broadway shows, as Little Jake in *Annie Get Your Gun*, Chip in *Beauty and the Beast*, Gavroche in *Les Misérables*, and Kurt in *The Sound of Music*.

It wasn't just his vocals that led to early success.

Nick's parents say he was blessed with charisma and likability.

Here's the SCOOP! Look for Nick's performances in *Beauty and the Beast*, *Les Misérables*, and *Annie Get Your Gun* on YouTube— you won't be disappointed.

Joe, the family comedian, was a little jealous, tbh. But then he nabbed some stage time of his own, allowing him to exercise those comedy chops. Nick was at an audition for *Oliver!* in Nyack, New York, when the director caught a glimpse of Joe, with his long, shaggy dark hair, and asked him to audition. Joe got the part of the Artful Dodger. (There's an adorable photo of him out there in top hat and tails.) And then in 2002, he landed a part in Baz Luhrmann's production of the opera *La Bohème* on Broadway.

All three boys were signed to a talent agent, and

their parents likely logged too many hours chauffeuring them to auditions. Not to be left out of the spotlight, Kevin—who wasn't interested in singing—scored some TV commercials. Luckily, Wyckoff isn't far from New York City. And their parents were game.

"My parents have sacrificed so much, more than any parents really should. And they're amazing, and we appreciate everything they've ever done for us and always will," Kevin told *J-14* back in 2007.

While Nick was in *Beauty and the Beast*, he and his dad wrote a song called "Joy to the World (A Christmas Prayer)" for the *Broadway's Greatest Gifts: Carols for a Cure, Vol. 4* album. The track was released to Christian radio stations, and Nick signed with a Christian music label and made a record. Unfortunately, the record didn't really take off as they had hoped.

But Nick and his brothers decided to write a song together: "Please Be Mine." It took them all of ten minutes. (They were seventeen, fifteen, and twelve at the time.) When the president of Columbia Records heard it, he loved it and signed the brothers as a group. You read that correctly. The first song they wrote together got them signed as a band!

Okay. You're thinking, *This all happened so fast . . . that's redonkulus!* In some ways, yes. But the road ahead would not be paved with gold right away.

First bump: What to call them? Some of the ideas thrown around: Sons of Jonas, Jonas3, Jonas Cubed, Run Jonas Run (Seriously???), and Jonas, Jonas, Jonas. They decided to just call themselves the Jonas Brothers. Phew! That could have gone badly . . .

With Kevin on lead guitar and Nick and Joe on vocals, the band started writing more and recording. And they hit the road, warming up for people like Jesse McCartney and the Backstreet Boys. But there wasn't much cash attached to those gigs, and the family was often financially strapped. Their first tour was in a van and a trailer, and sometimes they did quick round trips to places like Boston to avoid staying in hotels. They played a lot of mall food courts and schools, often for a few hundred people, if they were lucky.

They weren't allowed to tell anyone what they were doing because the church wouldn't have approved of them making music that wasn't Christian.

Their first single was "Mandy," named for a girl Joe had dated in high school. Not a Christian song. "Year 3000" actually became one of their biggest hits. That wasn't considered Christian, either. "Please Be Mine" was, of course, included on that first album, *It's About Time*, which is aptly named, because it took forever to come out. When it finally was released, it didn't pull in the kind of numbers they'd hoped for.

In the meantime, Kevin Sr. was forced to resign as pastor from the church, in part because the family was moving away from Christian music. (According to Joe in a 2013 interview, there was also a scandal around stolen church funds that divided the church.) It was devastating for the family, both socially and financially. Joe says it had an effect on the way he viewed the concept of church. Their lives were wrapped up in the church, and they had to move to another town in New Jersey—Little Falls—and into a smaller house.

In the new Jonas documentary, *Chasing Happiness*, the brothers go back to Wyckoff to check out their old house and the church. You can feel the film's mood shift as they drive by in the rain. They say it was a real blow to be rejected by the church they loved so much.

"It's rare that we go to a place that we're not accepted," Nick says to his brothers in the film. "It's like there's two buildings in the world that I can think of where we're told, 'No, you may not enter.' The house we grew up in and the church we helped build."

Adding fuel to the fire, Columbia Records dumped the Jonas Brothers after their album failed to take off. Not a happy time in the Jonas house. But out of the ashes came the seeds of success. In the basement of that house in Little Falls, they wrote a lot of songs.

In the end, Columbia's dismissal turned out to be a blessing in disguise. (Not for Columbia.) Because another big company was waiting to scoop up the band of brothers.

JONAS BASICS

NAME	KEVIN	JOE	NICK
BIRTHDAY	11/5/87	8/15/89	9/16/92
ZODIAC SIGN	Scorpio	Leo	Virgo
BIRTHPLACE	Teaneck, NJ	Casa Grande, AZ	Dallas, TX
EYE COLOR	Hazel	Brown	Brown
MIDDLE NAME	Kevin*	Adam	Jerry

★No, his parents weren't cruel enough to name him "Kevin Kevin." His real first name is actually Paul, but he goes by Kevin, just like his father does.

CHAPTER 2

DISNEY BROS

*T*hey weren't making Christian music, but their songs were still G-rated and so was their image. *Rolling Stone* magazine called them the "Clean Teen Machine." They were young, charming, talented, and cute—in that nice-boy-with-a-hint-of-rocker-edge way (Kevin and Joe flat-ironing their hair, Nick with that famous mop of curls). So what better fit for the Jonas Brothers than the Walt Disney Company, with its growing tween-to-teen audience? Disney showed up with a contract just after Columbia gave them the thumbs-down.

Right off the bat, big things started happening for the JoBros. They moved to Los Angeles, where they wrote songs and played music all day every day with professional musicians and producers. But not ones to fall behind academically, the brothers were homeschooled by their parents.

Soon Disney began airing their new videos, including the "Year 3000" video, between TV shows. Then the brothers guest-starred as themselves on an episode of *Hannah Montana*, setting a Disney record with 10.7 million viewers. And *BAM!* Just like that, their fan base exploded, catapulting them from opening act to headliners in just a few months. Suddenly, they were playing full arenas, armed with their new album, *Jonas Brothers*, and the singles "Hold On" and "S.O.S." The album sold nearly 2.5 million copies!

Here's a small SCOOP! Nick fell hard for Miley Cyrus when they guest-starred on *Hannah Montana*. Nick says he could finally write about love and know what it felt like.

In the *Chasing Happiness* documentary, there's footage of the first time it really sunk in how mega they were. It was at the Texas State Fair in 2007, where cars were backed up to Oklahoma waiting to see the Jonas Brothers! They'd been touring in Europe and didn't know they were blowing up in the United States.

Joe told *Vulture* it was off the hook! "There were forty thousand people, and we needed to get a helicopter in order to make it to the show because the traffic was so bad. I remember sitting in that helicopter, flying over all those cars, and thinking, *This is really happening."*

They were the modern-day Beatles, with packs of sobbing stans following them everywhere they went. It was exciting, but it could also be scary. They were doing a meet-and-greet in Spain and one hundred thousand people showed up. Joe says it was like a "zombie apocalypse"!

But, come on—it must have been amazing! Kevin says he couldn't get a single date in high school, and suddenly girls were swarming him and showing up uninvited in hotel rooms. Talk about being a stan . . . not cool!

Nick jokes in the *Chasing Happiness* documentary that the fandom had another effect. "I think my brothers and I became closest when we found a common ground beyond music and family: girls." There's even a great scene in the film with old footage in a car where Kevin is talking to a Danielle on the phone about meeting him after a show for a date. (Yes, that Danielle.) And his brothers tease him, saying it's his future wife on the phone. (Nailed it!)

And then there were the purity rings. The idea was to wear them to signify that they were waiting for the right person to have a physical relationship. The rings were a vestige of their religious life, something the guys say all their church friends wore back home in Wyckoff. But out of the church and in the public sphere, some people, like actor Russell Brand and the show *South Park* to name a few, roasted them for it. The brothers were the butt of a lot of jokes. And as Joe told James Corden in 2019 during an episode of "Carpool Karaoke," at a certain point, the rings started to feel ridiculous: "When you're, like, twelve and you do that, because we grew up . . . in a church and our dad was a pastor, and so, like, it kinda just came natural for everyone that we grew up with to go through this, and get one, and say I'm going to wait for the right person—some people say I'll wait till marriage—when you're about fifteen, sixteen you start dating, and you go, wait a minute—what did I . . . what did I say I was going to do? What did I say I was going to promise to do?"

There were definitely some trade-offs. But what Disney promised to do was make them into superstars, and the company delivered in spades. The success train was on track and moving at the speed of light. In 2008, the JoBros released another album called *A Little Bit Longer* and embarked on their *Look Me in the Eyes* tour in Europe and the

Burnin' Up summer tour in North America.

Next stop: *Camp Rock.* If you weren't alive in 2008, you have no clue what a massive deal this movie was for young fans of the Jonas Brothers and Demi Lovato, their costar. The plot goes like this: A teenage girl, played by Demi Lovato, wants to spend her summer at Camp Rock, but the only way she can afford to go is to work in the kitchen. When a teen pop star and heartthrob played by none other than Joe Jonas overhears her singing, he tries to find the girl behind the voice. It's *Cinderella* meets *The Little Mermaid* meets *School of Rock.* And it worked. (How could it possibly fail?) Fans loved it so much, Disney produced *Camp Rock 2: The Final Jam.* The movies helped seal the Jonases', as well as Demi's, cult status for tweens and teens.

The year 2009 brought another album, *Lines, Vines and Trying Times,* which debuted at number one on the *Billboard 200.* And then there was *Jonas,* the Disney TV show. It's a campy version of their lives, a goofy sitcom that was fun for their fans and painful for parents. The jokes were corny, but it was all about the eye candy and their relationships. In *Chasing Happiness*, Nick says he regrets doing season two of *Jonas* because it stunted their growth.

Problem was, it seems the Jonas Brothers were getting too old for Disney. They were still acting like boys on TV, but in 2009 Kevin was twenty-two, Joe was twenty, and Nick was seventeen. Kevin actually got married to Danielle that year! They were turning into men but trapped in a show that appealed to tweens . . . *awkward*

Nobody wants to look a gift mouse in the mouth, but all three Jonas Brothers were outgrowing their "clean teen machine" image, and something had to give.

SCOOP! QUIZ

ARE YOU A ROCKIN' CAMPER?

How much do you remember about *Camp Rock*?

⬇ **TAKE THIS SCOOP! QUIZ** ⬇
TO FIND OUT.

1. What is the name of the Jonases' fictional band? _____

_____

2. Who is Demi Lovato's character? _____

_____

_____

3. Who is Joe's character? _____

_____

_____

4. Where was *Camp Rock* filmed? _____

_____

_____

5. What color is Demi Lovato's character's bedroom? _____

_____

6. Who is Kevin's character? _____

_____

_____

_____

7. What's the title of the *Camp Rock* sequel?

_____

_____

_____

8. What food do Caitlyn and Tess throw at each other in the cafeteria? _____

_____

9. Who is Nick's character? _____

_____

_____

_____

10. What's the name of Demi's character's mom's company? _____

_____

_____

_____

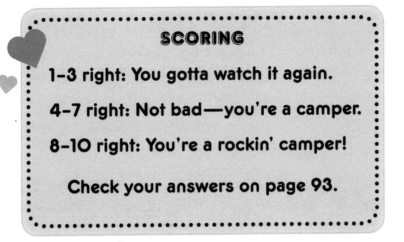

SCORING

1-3 right: You gotta watch it again.

4-7 right: Not bad—you're a camper.

8-10 right: You're a rockin' camper!

Check your answers on page 93.

CHAPTER 3

BREAKING UP

*L*et's fast-forward a bit, shall we? *Jonassing* is a full-time job. (Yes, that's a verb now.) So many tours, TV shows, documentaries, guest appearances—it would take more than one book to give you the deets on it all. But now we've come to that proverbial fork in the road where there's a major shift. The band is still together, Kevin Jonas is married to Danielle (Dani) Deleasa, a former hairdresser from New Jersey, and they're documenting it all in the E! series *Married to Jonas*.

The JoBros had been on hiatus since 2010. They hadn't made an album or gone on tour in over three years. In the meantime, Joe released his debut solo album, *Fastlife*, which only sold 45,000 copies by 2015, pretty much a flop by industry standards.

Nick made an album with his band, called Nick Jonas & the Administration. Their album didn't exactly kill, either. The lesson here? Hot boys don't always produce hot albums.

Nick also returned to his first love, the theater, and found success (and joy). He made his West End (the London equivalent of Broadway) debut in a new production of *Les Misérables*, this time playing Marius Pontmercy. He also played Link Larkin in *Hairspray* at the Hollywood Bowl for a few nights. He loved being back in the theater. (How much would you love to see him in a show?)

Then, as documented on *Married to Jonas,* it was time to make a fifth album and hit the road. Hiatus over, solo recording careers not taking off as some would hope, the brothers decided to go back to what they did best: making music together.

Here's the catch: The chemistry wasn't there. Something had changed, and Kevin, Joe, and Nick couldn't recapture the magic. Showing up on *Married to Jonas* wasn't helping, either.

"Our whole life was a closed-door meeting, and Kevin invited cameras into that meeting finally. We felt like he was going to air out a lot of our [stuff] that we didn't want people to know about," Joe says in *Chasing Happiness*.

But first . . . Let's talk musical theater!

ON *LES MISÉRABLES*

Les Misérables the musical is based on the historical novel of the same name by French author Victor Hugo. Published in 1862, it's considered one of the greatest novels of the nineteenth century. It is also one of the longest novels ever written: 1,900 pages in the original French version, 1,400 in English! It's a story of despair and war, crushingly sad at times, depressing in the accuracy of how women, children, and the poor were treated in France in the early nineteenth century.

Les Mis, as it is commonly known, was made into a musical that functions like an opera, with almost all the lines sung. It ran in London from 1985 to 2019, making it the longest running musical in London's West End. It has run on Broadway three different times, starting in 1987. In its first run, it won eight Tony Awards, including Best Musical. *Les Misérables* was also made into a movie starring Hugh Jackman and Anne Hathaway. Check it out!

But they plowed ahead, releasing the song "Meet You in Paris" and announcing a world tour in 2012–13. Their fifth studio album was scheduled to be released in 2013. The tour would start in October at Radio City Music Hall in New York City.

A few days before it was supposed to begin, the tour was abruptly canceled.

Behind the scenes, the Jonas family was in the throes of one of the most painful conversations of their lives.

Here's another small SCOOP! It was Nick who came to his dad and his brothers and said he didn't think they were connecting to the music, to their fans, or to one another. It was time, he said, for the Jonas Brothers to break up.

Clearly, it was heartbreaking: "I felt betrayed, I felt lied to, I felt angry, numb," Joe says in *Chasing Happiness*. "What hurt the most was that it came from Nick, because he is my best friend." It is heartbreaking, isn't it?

Looking back, Joe admits it was probably time, even if he couldn't see it then. In an interview with *Billboard* he said, "We were going through the motions, without the heart of it." It wasn't just the music that suffered. "The way we communicated to each other wasn't healthy anymore."

Kevin was devastated. And then there were the fans. It rocked the pop world, and everyone wanted to know what had happened to the inseparable brothers.

But every good thing must come to an end. And it was their time. So they canceled the making of their fifth album and set out to do their own things.

Nick went back into the studio and came out with two more albums over the next few years. You might know the singles "Jealous" and "Close," with singer Tove Lo. He was also nominated for a Golden Globe for his song "Home" from the animated film *Ferdinand*. Of course, there was no shortage of women in his life. (More on that later!) And he grew up. He was suddenly Nick Jonas, the man. No more curly mop.

Joe created the band DNCE with some friends and had a huge hit, "Cake by the Ocean," in 2015. The catchy, danceable song seemed to be on every radio station all the time. It had a strong debut and peaked at nine on the *Billboard 200* in the United States. Like his younger brother, Joe dated a number of women during this time, including supermodel Gigi Hadid. He also spent a chunk of his time in tattoo parlors. (More on that later, too!)

And Kevin was occupied with his growing family. He and Dani had their first daughter, Alena Rose Jonas, in February 2014. Their second daughter, Valentina Angelina Jonas, was born in October 2016. He also started the real-estate development and construction company Jonas/Werner Fine

Custom Homes and became co-CEO of the communications company The Blu Market.

So, nobody was slacking. They were all hitting their stride. But their sibling relationships had suffered from the breakup, and there was some major repair work to do. That's next.

CHAPTER 4

REUNITED AND IT FEELS SO "COOL"

*T*he Jonas split dragged on for six years. That's a lifetime in the music industry. Did their fans miss them? Did the world give two pom-poms if the Jonas Brothers ever made another record?

The answer turned out to be a resounding yas! on both counts. Comebacks are tricky business: Sometimes they work, and sometimes they fail miserably (see: Lindsay Lohan). The Jonas Brothers were ready. But it wasn't as simple as jetting back to the studio.

"Basically, about a year ago . . . we started talking about making a documentary together . . . just to tell our story, you know, childhood into our career together," Nick told late-night host James Corden.

"And in that process, you know, we did some very necessary healing cause, you know, when things ended, it wasn't the best . . . In that, we started saying that there was a magic when we were together that we would all love to feel again."

Maybe it's irony, maybe it makes perfect sense, but it was Nick who broached the subject of reuniting. (Remember, he was the one who split them up.) Kevin says his younger bro casually said he missed playing music with his family. Kevin was pumped at the thought of his daughters seeing the band perform for the first time. Joe was less convinced—but eventually he came around.

Here's the SCOOP! They tried to keep it a secret—both the documentary and the new album they were recording. But Kevin's daughter Alena spilled the tea at school one day!

So, how do you heal? Nick and Joe moved in

together for a while. Kevin's kids helped bring the brothers closer. And there were multiple convos and some difficult truths for each of them to swallow, after years of stuffing their feelings. Making *Chasing Happiness* forced the Jonases to face up to the resentment and disappointments they'd been holding on to. They didn't do the hard psych work in a therapist's office, but rather one night out on the town in Australia when Kevin and Nick were visiting Joe, who was Down Under judging that country's *The Voice.* (Don't try this at home, kids.) And it was revealing.

Kevin and Joe were hurt that Nick pulled the plug on the band. Kevin was hurt that Joe and Nick played a concert without him. It all came tumbling out. But they were united around the idea that no matter how much success each found on his own, there was a beautiful magic they had together that couldn't be replicated on a solo stage. (Hey, your fans could have told you that a long time ago!)

During the break, Joe and Nick both got married, and Nick told Jimmy Fallon that now they all have personal muses to help them write the songs they want to sing.

"I think we looked a long time for the kind of inspiration that we now have, whether it's kids or wives and fans, you know, also this journey we went on together over the course of a year and a half, two years of making the film together, coming back together, it's all in there. But, you know, it's the best thing in the world to be able to write a love letter to your wife in the musical form." What a romantic!

The Jonases say they were jamming together in Cuba, playing "Lovebug" from 2008, when they realized how happy they were to be making music together again.

While the brothers were getting in touch with all of their feels, their new record company, Republic, was psyched to get them back into the studio and on the road. Republic's Wendy Goldstein told

Billboard, "As a record executive, this is the thing you dream [about]: a fully functional, hitting-on-all-cylinders recording artist that has a history, has a catalog, has contemporary current hits, is in the mix." She added, "I knew if we did this right, this is the gift that keeps on giving: a world tour, many more albums, solo records again at some point."

So far, it's all been cool, which is the title of one of the first singles off their new album. (More on that later!) But first, it's time to get personal.

Here's a small (wholesome) SCOOP! The family-oriented Jonas Brothers always try to wrap up their writing/ recording sessions by dinnertime, which is not the norm in the music biz, where bands often stay up all night working.

CHAPTER 5

J SISTERS

Time for a little detour. This chapter will be painful for some of you, and you might want to skip it altogether if you're madly in love with one (or more) of the Jonases. Because as you must already know, they are all officially off the market. And this chapter is about the women responsible for that.

You can take comfort in this: all three Jonases married well. As different as their wives are, they share something in common: They appear to be deeply in love with their husbands and supportive of their careers.

There was, however, some gossip about them not getting along. Haters gonna hate. Some websites broadcast tension between Priyanka and Danielle, claiming Danielle was the odd girl out. Or that Sophie and Danielle didn't like Priyanka. But if Instagram means anything (and it does, duh!), the sisters are buds. Sophie and Priyanka probably have more in common since they're both actors, but that doesn't mean Danielle gets left behind. And they all call one another the J Sisters . . . but you already knew that, didn't you? Neither Sophie nor Priyanka have sisters, and Priyanka says it's been great to gain them through marriage.

⬇ HERE ARE THE MARRIAGE DEETS ⬇

Kevin and Danielle

Danielle Deleasa was born in 1986, which makes her older than Kevin. Even though they both grew up in New Jersey, she met the oldest Jonas while on vacation in the Bahamas in 2007. The story goes that she was walking down the beach with a flower in her hair, and Kevin took notice. She claims she didn't know who the Jonas Brothers were. (Come on—how is that possible?)

One night after a Jonas Brothers concert in Vancouver, Kevin flew to New Jersey to propose to Danielle with a three-carat ring. (That's pretty big, in case you didn't know.) Their wedding took place on Long Island during a blizzard! They live in New Jersey with their two adorable daughters. If you want to see more of Kevin and Danielle, check out old episodes of *Married to Jonas*.

How about an extra SCOOP!? Danielle grew up with two sisters and one brother. After high school, she became a hairdresser. Now she designs jewelry. Her company has two lines of affordable jewelry: Moments and Essentials.

Joe and Sophie

Sophie Turner was born in England in 1996. She may be younger than Joe (by six and a half years), but she's got a couple of inches on him. Sophie is a megastar in her own right. She was one of the main characters on the HBO TV series *Game of Thrones*, playing the powerful and beautiful Sansa Stark for eight seasons. You could say she grew up on the show—it started filming when she was just fourteen.

The way Joe and Sophie met might surprise you: on Instagram. They had friends who thought they should meet, and then Joe DM'd her. They went Instagram official in 2017 when Sophie posted a photo of Joe on a boat in Miami. They were still pretty mum about their relationship until they posted their engagement on Insta. The two first tied the knot in Vegas, then at a chateau in the South of France in the summer of 2019. Their timing was lousy: It was the hottest day on record for the country, according to TV therapist Dr. Phil, who was a guest. (What's with the Jonases and bad-weather weddings?)

Here's a small **SCOOP!** Joe and Sophie's Vegas ceremony was conducted by an Elvis impersonator!

And an extra **SCOOP!** . . . just cuz Sophie and Joe are friends with TV therapist Dr. Phil. On his *Phil in the Blanks* podcast, Sophie very bravely told Dr. Phil that she has suffered from depression for five or six years and that there were times when she found it difficult to get out of bed. An emotional Sophie explained that social media could be a catalyst, especially once she became famous. "It was just a lot of weight comments, or I would have spotty skin because I was a teenager— and that's normal—and I used to get a lot of comments about my skin and my weight and how I wasn't a good actress." And Sophie said she believed them.

Nick and Priyanka

Priyanka Chopra (sounds like "Oprah") was also famous long before she met Nick. Born in 1982 in India, Priyanka is ten years older than her husband. Like Joe and Sophie, she and Nick met through social media. Nick says they were connected by friends and started communicating via text. It took a while for them to actually get together in person, and their first big outing was at the Met Gala. (More on that below!) And then some time went by before they got together again. But when they did, Nick told Jimmy Fallon, it stuck. "It was kind of immediate, and we just knew it was right and jumped right in. And we're very happy."

When they got engaged, Nick and Priyanka flew to India with Nick's parents for the traditional Roka ceremony, which celebrates the union of the bride and groom's families. That was just the beginning. Nick and Priyanka had both Christian and Hindu wedding ceremonies in India, plus three receptions! That's a lot of (stunning) wedding dresses, including a custom Ralph Lauren white gown (with 11,632 Swarovski crystals and a seventy-five-foot-long veil) and a traditional red Indian gown. Nick even wore a turban for one of the ceremonies!

EXTRA SCOOP! Priyanka was an excellent student and hoped to study aeronautical engineering and work for NASA. But that all changed in 2000, when she was crowned Miss World! After that, the film industry came calling, and she answered. Priyanka appeared in a number of films in India and later became famous in the United States with her lead role in the TV series *Quantico*. She made her Hollywood film debut in the movie *Baywatch*. Priyanka is also a Goodwill Ambassador for UNICEF.

Sometimes the sisters steal the show—in a good way! When the Jonas Brothers surprised their fans with a concert at a bar at Penn State University, the crowd started chanting "Lady Stark" for Sophie, in reference to her *GOT* character. And in the video for the band's 2019 single "Sucker," the beautiful

Jonas wives take center stage.

More on "Sucker" and the Jonas Brothers' 2019 comeback, next.

But first . . .
Let's talk fashion!

HERE'S THE SCOOP!

ON THE MET GALA

You may have seen celebrities dressed in couture or wacky fashion to go to the Met Gala. What is that, you ask? Its formal name is the Costume Institute Gala, and its purpose is to raise money for the Metropolitan Museum of Art's Costume Institute in New York City. And it's quite glamorous.

Every spring, celebrities from the fashion world, music business, film, and television attend the gala. Each year the event has a different theme, and guests are expected to dress accordingly. And like the Oscars, the paparazzi photograph and broadcast stars in their incredible outfits as they walk the red carpet. *Vogue* Editor-in-Chief Anna Wintour is the chair of the gala, which raises millions of dollars every year.

CHAPTER 6

HAPPY NOW

*B*ack together and feeling settled in their personal lives, Kevin, Joe, and Nick were pumped to recapture the magic of their earlier days. But it would be different this time: no more Disney or the restraints that came with it.

Nick had become a man—and a ripped one, at that! Joe found his edge with DNCE and a slew of tattoos. (More on that later!) Kevin went deep into family mode and emerged even hotter and more confident. He seriously glowed up.

And can we talk about their hair??? Gone were those shaggy mop-tops we initially fell in love with. The brothers were clean-cut this time around. Even their wardrobe was more mature, as they wore more adventurous, often bright, and whimsical clothes. You can even catch Nick wearing a monochromatic pink suit with white sneakers.

Most importantly, when the brothers returned to the studio, they found a new sound that they could all embrace.

"I think we were able to craft a sound early on which really describes the sound of the project," Nick told *Wonderland* magazine. "It's a real combination of what Joe did with DNCE, what I was able to do with my solo stuff, and combining those with elements that are just classic Jonas Brothers."

Take "Sucker," the first hit of their new album, *Happiness Begins*. There's the DNCE dance vibe, cool bass rock beat, the clapping, and Joe's sultry vocals. Then enter Nick with his pop vocals and lyrics. And yet, somehow, it's classic Jonas Brothers. Even after all these years, they're still the harmonizing pop heartthrobs that catapulted into the stratosphere more than a decade ago.

"Sucker" is the first Jonas Brothers song to hit

number one on the *Billboard Hot 100*! Clearly, they've got the recipe for success down. All those years, all those songs, but none ever reached the number-one spot until the comeback of all comebacks delivered this one and its campy video, costarring who else but their wives.

Here's a single SCOOP! for you . . . The closest the Jonas Brothers got to the number-one Billboard spot before "Sucker" was "Burnin' Up," which reached the number-five spot.

Kevin told *Wonderland* that their personal lives have had an effect on the creation of this album. "It was a little bit of trial and error, which was a nice change. I think back then we'd walk in and all be in different places in our lives when we'd write songs—one person was going through a breakup, one person had someone new in their lives—but now we're all in similar places in our personal lives, so it helps when it comes to writing music, we can all really lean towards each other and also know when an idea is better than yours."

The other early single release was "Cool," a chill, tongue-in-cheek pop song that could be the Jonas Brothers' comeback anthem. How about that lyric, "Is it me, or am I just havin' a good year?" (Uh, yeah, you are.) It's also a showcase for clever, self-referential lyrics, aka, it's funny:

> **Oh, I feel like Post Malone when I get home**
> **Sittin' there, winnin' like it's *Game of Thrones***
> **And now that we've made it, how complicated**
> **was last year?**
>
> ◀◀ ❙❙ ▶▶

That verse was sung by Joe, of course.

The combo of what they've learned from their solo careers—coupled with that classic Jonas Brothers charm—was on stage at the Billboard Music Awards, where they did a medley of "Jealous," "Cake by the Ocean," and "Sucker."

And who was right there in the front row? The three women in their lives: Danielle, Sophie, and Priyanka.

Just days before the Jonas Brothers dropped *Happiness Begins*, they released their *Chasing Happiness* documentary. Interestingly enough, though, the documentary gets pretty serious and isn't always light and love. The brothers get real about what they went through, what happened to them, and they peel back some of the scars of that early rift with the church. These guys can go deep!

But ultimately, now that they're back together, performing and touring—and selling out Madison Square Garden—Kevin says they just want to have a little fun.

"In the current state of the world, everything is so serious all the time, and it's nice to be put out of that for a minute and just enjoy the fun. That's kind of where we're at."

You can't help but have fun listening to their new album: tracks like "Only Human," with its reggae beat, or "Don't Throw It Away," with its slammin' falsetto chorus.

The releases didn't stop with the documentary, album, and videos . . . there was also a book, a memoir written by the trio called *Blood*, released a few months later.

Who knows what's next? But you know with all the success coming their way as Jonas 2.0, there will be more.

CHAPTER 7

JUST KEVIN

*K*evin has always been the underrated Jonas. If Nick and Joe were the front men/heart-throbs, Kevin was the other Jonas, the family man, the one in the background. But that all changed with the 2019 Jonaissance.

Some people peak in high school, some in college. But some peak later. There's been a lot of talk about Kevin's glow up. People are taking notice of Kevin's adorable daddy videos, his more chiseled face, and those jacked arms. All those hot guitar-playing pics on Instagram next to the family pics at the beach. And he's still the nice guy he's always been.

The Scorpio: Kevin is a true Scorpio, a leader. So you probably think of Nick as the leader of the band, and in the obvious ways, he is. But Kevin has always been the eldest looking out for his kid brothers, and that will never change. He was considered the businessman of the group, too. Scorpios know what they want and aren't afraid to go after it. In both his career and personal life, Kevin has been true to his sign. Scorpios can also be stubborn and jealous, which is why they've gotta find the right love matches. Cancers and Virgos take note: You're the best love matches for Scorpio. And guess what? Danielle Jonas is a Virgo. Perfect.

The Family Man: Dani and daughters Alena and Valentina are all over Kevin's Instagram page. In August 2019, he posted a pic of his forearm with a new tattoo of a bunny-and-bear sketch with the story, "Love bringing reminders of my girls with me everywhere I go!" In other photos, you can see his daughters often have their bunny and bear stuffed animals with them. He posted Alena's first day of kindergarten, photos of him cuddling with his girls, kissing Danielle, with his family at home, and a video of him playing guitar for his daughter. On *The Tonight Show Starring Jimmy Fallon*, Kevin raved about having kids. "It's the best thing ever," he said.

The Guitar Player: Kevin started playing guitar when he was home sick from school for a week and got bored. He was tired of watching lame TV shows, so he picked up a copy of a "teach yourself guitar" book that was in the house, and once he started learning, he never put down the guitar again. Kevin plays electric, bass, and acoustic guitar. His first guitar was a 1969 Gibson Les Paul Gold Top, and Kevin says he's remained a Les Paul guy.

The Actor and Reality Star: Kevin has appeared on TV and in films a lot. It all started with those commercials in the early days, before the Jonas Brothers were a thing. They appeared together on *Hannah Montana* and in the *Camp Rock* movies, where Kevin played the guitarist Jason. Kevin starred with his brothers in the Disney show *Jonas*, which ran for two seasons, and Kevin and Danielle starred in their own E! reality series, *Married to Jonas*, which also ran for two seasons. Kevin was in the seventh season of *Celebrity Apprentice*.

Here's a small SCOOP! Kevin was the leader of his team when they lost in the second episode of *Celebrity Apprentice*.

A Man in Touch with His Feelings: Kevin admits he was depressed after the band broke up in 2013. No kidding. They were about to tour again, and then, suddenly, they weren't. Jonas fans were upset, so you can only imagine how the band members were feeling. Kevin told New York's Z100 Radio that it was tough to come down from the adrenaline rush of being in the limelight.

"When the Jonas Brothers went dark, we went dark. We didn't do a single interview, we didn't talk to anybody, we just went dark. I just got really depressed for a while. There's a mourning process."

Luckily, he had Danielle to help him get through it, and then Alena, who was born in 2014.

Okay, how about a reading break? Pencils out! It's time for a SCOOP! Quiz . . .

SCOOP! QUIZ

HOW WELL DO *YOU* KNOW KEVIN?

It seems like everyone knows everything about Joe and Nick. But not so much about Kevin . . .

So, how well do *you* know the oldest Jonas?

⬇ TAKE THIS SCOOP! QUIZ ⬇ TO FIND OUT!

1. What sports did Kevin play in high school? _____

_____

_____

_____

2. How old was Kevin when he married Danielle? _____

3. How did Kevin fracture his shoulder at seventeen? _____

_____

_____

_____

4. Name the instruments Kevin plays. ___

_____

_____

_____

5. What's the name of the food app Kevin created? _____

_____

_____

_____

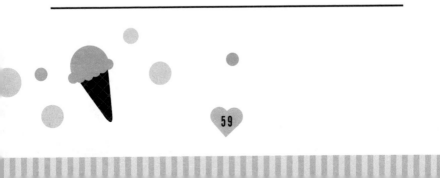

6. On which TV show did Kevin appear as himself as a building contractor? _____

_____

_____

_____

7. In the "Sucker" cover art, Kevin is wearing a colorful Dries Van Noten shirt. Which famous female singer wore the same shirt? _____

_____

8. On which reality show was Kevin the second contestant to go home? _____

_____

_____

9. Why was Kevin home from school the first time he picked up a guitar? _____

_____

_____

10. What electronic toy did Kevin do a TV commercial for? _____

_____

_____

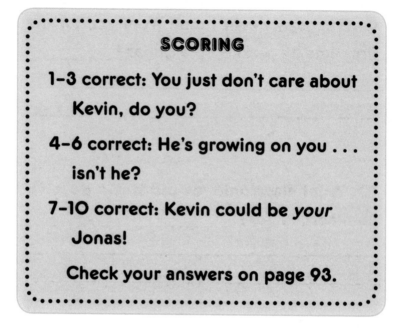

SCORING

1–3 correct: You just don't care about Kevin, do you?

4–6 correct: He's growing on you . . . isn't he?

7–10 correct: Kevin could be *your* Jonas!

Check your answers on page 93.

CHAPTER 8

JUST JOE

Have you been in love with Joe Jonas as far back as you can remember? Or are you just falling now? He's always been the stylish brother with the sexy voice, and now that he's married to actor Sophie Turner, he might just be the most-envied one. Joe Jonas is cool—and his style is continually evolving. Here's everything you need to know about the middle Jonas.

The DNCE Front Man: In interviews, Joe has talked a lot about how he felt suffocated by Disney as he got older. He really broke free of that kid-pop universe when he started playing with DNCE. (The band name is *dance* misspelled.) He drops the F-bomb in the huge DNCE hit "Cake by the Ocean," and the video features lots of women in bikinis. BTW, did you know that the band worked on that song with Swedish producers who kept confusing "cake by the ocean" for "sex on the beach," which is the name of a drink? That's how the song, which reached the top ten on several charts, got its name. DNCE has three members in addition to Joe: drummer Jack Lawless, bassist/keyboardist Cole Whittle, and guitarist JinJoo Lee. The band is on hiatus while the brothers tour.

The Punk: In Joe's words, as told to *Vulture*: "I was a pastor's kid, so eyes were always on me, even then. I sat in the first pew of the church, and I had to wear a suit every Sunday, because my parents wanted me to be this role model that I didn't always want to be. I preferred going to punk-rock shows in small venues in New Jersey, where we grew up, wearing my jean jacket and all my band pins. That's how I fell in love with music, how I became obsessed with it. I'd stand there, watching the singer running around the stage, owning the crowd. I didn't even notice whatever else was happening onstage. All I could see was the singer."

The Always-Stylish Bro: All the Jonas Brothers have style, and Joe really brings it. He was the most stylish one back in the early days, with that ironed hair. All three looked like vampires at one point, with their pale skin and dark hair, but Joe rocked it. (Kevin tried to straighten his hair, but it never really worked.) Why the 'do? Joe told Jimmy Fallon he was trying to emulate the lead singer of a German band called Tokio Hotel. Now he wears his hair more naturally, but it's always well coiffed. Joe is all about his sneakers, skinny jeans, leather and denim jackets, and suits and ties. He seems to like the fully buttoned-up shirt look, too. And there are lots of shots of Joe and Sophie on Instagram looking Hollywood glam in black tie and other party attire.

The Dog Bro: Joe and Sophie had two Alaskan Klee Kais (think small huskies), Waldo Picasso and Porky Basquiat, named for the artists Picasso and Basquiat. (See the art history SCOOP! on page 71.) Sadly, Waldo Picasso was killed in a freak car accident in New York City. Porky Basquiat has his own Instagram page with 144K followers and a cheeky sense of humor. If you like adorable pups (and who doesn't?), you need to follow. Porky was even part of Joe's wedding party in France. Naturally, he wore a suit and bow tie.

The Former Boyfriend: Joe has been linked to a number of women, including some celebrities. Famously, he dated Taylor Swift for a few months in 2008 before breaking up with her over the phone in a twenty-seven-second call (*ouch!*). That breakup was evidently inspiration for the Swift song "Forever and Always." (You never want to get on her bad side.) Joe dated Demi Lovato for a few months while they were filming *Camp Rock*. Once again, he broke it off. (Are we sensing a theme here?) It was tough for him because Demi was struggling with drug abuse at the time. But they remained friends. Joe dated actor Ashley Greene for nearly a year in 2010–11, and of course he was heartbroken when they split. Joe briefly dated model Gigi Hadid, but right after they broke up she chose another direction with singer Zayn Malik.

The Lion: Joe was born August 15, 1989, which makes him a Leo. His element is fire (duh!). Leos are creative, generous, and humorous. They're also known to be warmhearted and passionate. On the downside, they can be stubborn. Like Scorpios, Leos are natural-born leaders. Leo is most compatible with Aquarius and Gemini. Sophie Turner was born on February 21, which makes her a Pisces by one day. If she had been born on the twentieth, she'd be an Aquarius. Close enough, right?

SCOOP! EXTRA

A GUIDE TO JOE'S INK

Joe Jonas loves him some ink. Here are the deets on what some of his tattoos are and what they mean:

1. **A dog:** For Joe and Sophie's dog, Waldo Picasso, who died

2. **A three-point crown:** Could this be for the artist Basquiat (see page 71) and Joe's dog of the same name?

3. **A knot of two ropes:** The two ropes represent his parents, and the four ends, him and his brothers.

4. **West African Adrinka symbol:** It reportedly means, "Help me and let me help you."

5. **A slice of cake:** for "Cake by the Ocean"

6. Triangle with hand inside: He loves the number three because of his brothers; the hand is Mother Nature.

7. Lyrics of the song "Mr. Blue Sky" by Jeff Lynne:

> "Sun is shinin' in the sky
> There ain't a cloud in sight
> It's stopped rainin' everybody's in a play
> And don't you know
> It's a beautiful new day"

◀◀ ❚❚ ▶▶

8. A bird: Who knows?

9. An arrow: He and Nick got matching tattoos. Could it mean moving forward together?

10. A portrait of his grandfather

11. *The Persistence of Memory*: A Salvador Dalí painting

12. A seated woman: Joe insists it's not Sophie.

13. The number fifteen: He and Sophie got engaged on October 15.

14. "To Infinity": Joe got these words on his wrist; Sophie got "& Beyond" on hers.

15. A face with a dove: This is a Picasso drawing.

16. An ax: Any guesses?

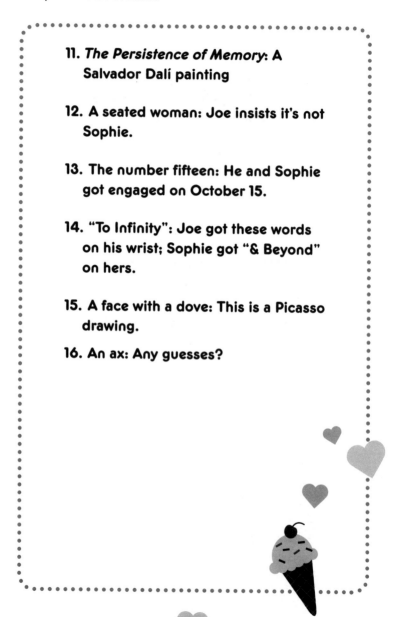

ON ART HISTORY

Clearly, Joe is a fan of ink and a fan of art. Here's the SCOOP! on two famous artists who have inspired Joe:

Pablo Picasso was a Spanish artist who spent most of his adult life in France. He was incredibly prolific. According to Guinness World Records, by the time he died at age ninety-one, Picasso had created 13,500 paintings, one hundred thousand prints and engravings, 34,000 book illustrations, and 300 sculptures and ceramics! He is best known for his Cubist paintings. If you want to learn more about his personal life, a good book to read is *Life with Picasso*, by Françoise Gilot (although it does cover some adult topics). His partner for a long time, Gilot is the mother of Claude and Paloma Picasso, and a great artist in her own right.

Jean-Michel Basquiat was an American painter, graffiti artist, and musician born in Brooklyn, New York, in 1960. His father was Haitian and his mother was a New Yorker of Puerto Rican descent. When Basquiat was seventeen, he dropped out of school, and his father kicked him out of the house. He survived by selling sweatshirts and post-cards with his drawings. Basquiat was known as one of the leading artists of Neo-Expressionism, which refocused on the human form and other recogniz-able objects, often in colorful, violent, and emo-tional ways. A crown often appears in Basquiat's work on the heads of black athletes, musicians, and writers, elevating them to saintly status. Basquiat died at the age of twenty-seven.

CHAPTER 9

JUST NICK

*Y*ou love the confident smile. You melt when he tilts his head and looks into the camera. You're all about the *Midway* mustache. There's a lot to love about Nick Jonas. And he's all grown up. Nick was always the cute one, the baby of the family. (Well, not counting Frankie.) But now some would argue he's the hottest Jonas. He's got the swagger, the abs and arms, and that I'm-the-coolest-guy-in-the-room way of looking at the camera. Hey, if you've got it, flaunt it, right? It's not just his looks. The man has got some serious talent! The last couple of years, Nick has been hitting it out of the park.

The Movie Star and Entrepreneur: You'd think it would be enough that Nick is a rock star and

Broadway star. But, no. This guy is always up for the next thing, and he found it onscreen. He rocked it in *Jumanji: Welcome to the Jungle* and then took it up another notch in *Midway,* playing Bruno P. Gaido, a World War II gunner who was heroic in the Battle of Midway. He's also gone into business with the clothing designer John Varvatos. They're selling Villa One, a premium tequila. (Not until you're twenty-one.) And 2019 was the year Nick graced the cover of *Cigar Aficionado* magazine.

The Style Risk Taker: Speaking of fire, the man likes to make a statement with his clothes. Nick Jonas has come a long way from the kid in polo shirts and sweats. He still likes his sneakers. He also likes boots, especially Chelsea boots. And dress shoes. The guy likes shoes, period. His brothers say he is a shoe collector. And don't even try to steal his clothes, because he's very protective of them. (You can relate, right?) He looks fabulous in a tux, even better when it's white tie, and he can rock a monochromatic suit. And like Joe, he loves his jackets—especially the leather variety. Nick is not afraid to go bold with colors or patterns, and it all works. And does anyone look cooler in aviator sunglasses?

The Virgo: The Virgo man is hardworking and practical. Okay—that makes sense. Nick certainly works hard for a man who could sit back and relax if he wanted to. Virgos don't like to leave anything to chance. (Remember when Nick broke up the band? He didn't want to leave his career to chance.) Virgos lead an organized life. Priyanka says Nick's (very cool and modern) house in LA is super organized and neat. Like obsessively so. Speaking of Priyanka, she's a Cancer. And guess which signs are most compatible with Virgo? Yup. Cancer and Pisces.

The Details of His Disease: You probably know that Nick has type 1 diabetes. He's not shy about it. In the documentary *Chasing Happiness,* Kevin says they were on the road touring in the early days, before Disney, when Kevin saw Nick change his shirt and realized how thin he was—that he could see his brother's ribs. It turns out he was barely one hundred pounds. His parents say his personality was also changing—he was moody. And he was always thirsty, always had to go to the bathroom. The doctor sent him to a hospital, where he was given the diagnosis. Type 1 diabetes is a chronic condition in which the pancreas produces little or no insulin, resulting in elevated levels of sugar in the blood and urine. Nick is an inspiration to young people who are just finding out they have the disease. He's healthy—and in control of his body now. Plus, he has a great attitude about it. (And you love those Cigna body and mind commercials, yes?)

The Man with the Money: *Money* magazine estimates that Nick is the brother with the most cash, based on public records, real estate transactions, and news reports. The magazine put his net worth at around $25 million. Not bad, Nick. Not bad.

THE GHOSTS OF GIRLFRIENDS PAST: A (BRIEF) TIMELINE OF NICK'S EXES

"The course of true love never did run smooth." Those are famous words from William Shakespeare. And before finding true love with Priyanka, Nick had some bumpy parts on his path to her.

1. Miley Cyrus

Nick and Miley connected when the Jonas Brothers appeared on *Hannah Montana*. Kevin says his brother's head exploded when he met Miley! The two were just thirteen when they started dating, so how serious was it really going to get? But they did go out for about a year. So cute. And they each wrote a tune about the other: the Jonas Brothers' song "Wedding Bells" and Miley's "7 Things."

2. Selena Gomez

Staying within the Disney franchise, Nick dated Selena for just about two months.

3. Delta Goodrem

Nick's first relationship with an older woman. Nick was eighteen and the Australian singer, songwriter, and actor was twenty-six. They dated for about a year.

4. Olivia Culpo

This relationship hung on the longest until Priyanka took that title. Speaking of titles, Olivia is one of those celebs who's hard to label—let's just say she's a media influencer and TV reality star. And she was once Miss Universe. Now that's a serious title! Nick met her when he cohosted the Miss USA pageant. They dated for two years, and Nick's song "Jealous" is about her. She even starred in the video.

5. Lily Collins

The British actor made a brief appearance in Nick's life, but they only really dated a few times.

6. Kate Hudson

Nick underscored his interest in older women when he dated the actress and athletic-wear proprietor. She was thirty-six, and he was just twenty-three! It didn't last too long . . . maybe a summer? And they never went public.

7. Georgia Fowler

The Victoria's Secret model dated Nick for a short time. Nick even took her to his brother Joe's engagement party. But the relationship never cemented.

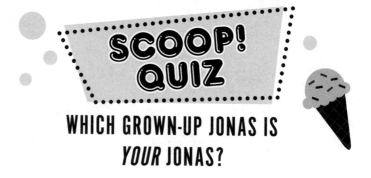

SCOOP! QUIZ

WHICH GROWN-UP JONAS IS *YOUR* JONAS?

Circle True or False. Then turn to page 94 to see how many "true" matches you got with each Jonas brother.

1. You love the color pink.   T F

2. You're a homebody.   T F

3. You're obsessed with shoes.   T F

4. You're a dog lover.   T F

5. You love travel and adventure.   T F

6. You think loyalty is the most important trait.   T F

7. You love the underdog.   T F

8. You sing Broadway show tunes in the car.   T F

9. You love Elvis impersonators.   T F

10. You think anyone over thirty is old.   T F

11. You can't wait to have kids.   T F

12. Your significant other has to be funny.   T F

SCOOP! QUIZ

SO YOU THINK YOU KNOW THE JONAS BROTHERS?

*T*ake this **SCOOP!** ultimate Jonas Brothers Quiz . . .

⬇ TO FIND OUT! ⬇

1. Which Jonas played the Artful Dodger in a stage version of *Oliver!*?

NICK   JOE   KEVIN   FRANKIE

2. Which Jonas has the largest shoe collection?

NICK   JOE   KEVIN   FRANKIE

3. Which Jonas dated Selena Gomez?

NICK   JOE   KEVIN   FRANKIE

4. Who got married on Long Island?

NICK   JOE   KEVIN   FRANKIE

5. Which Jonas dated Taylor Swift?

NICK   JOE   KEVIN   FRANKIE

6. Who won a Teen Choice Award for Choice TV Breakout Star Male?

NICK   JOE   KEVIN   FRANKIE

7. Which Jonas has a key tattooed on his arm?

NICK   JOE   KEVIN   FRANKIE

8. Whose first wedding ceremony was in Vegas?

NICK   JOE   KEVIN   FRANKIE

9. Who was nominated for Nickelodeon awards for Favorite TV actor?

NICK   JOE   KEVIN   FRANKIE

10. Who was a voice actor in the animated film *Ponyo*?

NICK   JOE   KEVIN   FRANKIE

11. Which Jonas was born in Teaneck, NJ?

NICK   JOE   KEVIN   FRANKIE

12. Which Jonas was born in Casa Grande, AZ?

NICK   JOE   KEVIN   FRANKIE

13. Which Jonas met his wife while vacationing in the Bahamas?

NICK   JOE   KEVIN   FRANKIE

14. Which Jonas was born in Ridgewood, NJ?

NICK   JOE   KEVIN   FRANKIE

15. Which Jonas was born in Dallas, TX?

NICK   JOE   KEVIN   FRANKIE

16. Which Jonas is still upset about the ballerina who trash-talked him?

NICK   JOE   KEVIN   FRANKIE

17. Which Jonas dated Kate Hudson?

NICK   JOE   KEVIN   FRANKIE

18. Which Jonas says he often gets mistaken for his brothers?

NICK   JOE   KEVIN   FRANKIE

19. Whose wife "judged a book by its cover" when she first met her future husband?

NICK   JOE   KEVIN   FRANKIE

20. Which Jonas leaves his wife love notes when he's traveling with the band?

NICK   JOE   KEVIN   FRANKIE

21. Who wrote the song "S.O.S."?

NICK   JOE   KEVIN   FRANKIE

22. Which Jonas was born on their parents' wedding anniversary?

NICK   JOE   KEVIN   FRANKIE

23. Which Jonas appeared in Baz Luhrmann's *La Bohème*?

NICK   JOE   KEVIN   FRANKIE

24. Which Jonas said he would like to be a race-car driver?

NICK   JOE   KEVIN   FRANKIE

25. Who lives in Beverly Hills?

NICK   JOE   KEVIN   FRANKIE

WRITE YOUR OWN SCOOP!

With the release of *Happiness Begins*, the Jonas Brothers have now released five studio albums. Rank your favorite albums here and write why you love each one.

1 _____

_____

2 _____

_____

3 _____

_____

4 _____

_____

5 _____

_____

You run into Nick, Kevin, and Joe in a coffee shop, and they invite you to sit down with them. What three questions do you ask them?

1. _____

_____

_____

2. _____

_____

_____

3. _____

_____

_____

The Jonas Brothers are putting on a concert and they need your help with the set list! What ten songs do you want to hear them play?

1 _____

2 _____

3 _____

4 _____

5 _____

6 _____

7 _____

8 _____

9 _____

10 _____

Now they want to bring out a special musical guest for the encore. Name the three musical artists you'd like to see them perform the final song with. Why?

1 _____

_____

_____

2 _____

_____

_____

3 _____

_____

_____

And what's the song they sing?

ANSWER KEY

♥ ♥ ♥

ARE YOU A ROCKIN' CAMPER?
1. Connect 3
2. Mitchie Torres
3. Shane Gray
4. YMCA Camp Wanakita, Haliburton, Canada, and Kilcoo Camp, Minden, Ontario
5. Purple
6. Jason Gray
7. *Camp Rock 2: The Final Jam*
8. Spaghetti
9. Nate Gray
10. Connie's Catering

HOW WELL DO YOU KNOW KEVIN?
1. Pole vaulting and water polo
2. Twenty-two
3. Skateboarding
4. Guitar, keyboard, mandolin, and drums
5. Yood
6. *The Real Housewives of New Jersey*
7. Beyoncé
8. *Celebrity Apprentice*

9. He had strep throat.
10. e•Brain

WHICH GROWN-UP JONAS IS *YOUR* JONAS?

1. Nick
2. Kevin
3. Nick
4. Joe
5. Joe
6. Kevin
7. Kevin
8. Nick
9. Joe
10. Nick
11. Kevin
12. Joe

SCOOP! ULTIMATE JONAS BROTHERS QUIZ

1. Joe
2. Nick
3. Nick
4. Kevin
5. Joe
6. Frankie
7. Kevin
8. Joe
9. Nick and Joe

10. Frankie
11. Kevin
12. Joe
13. Kevin
14. Frankie
15. Nick
16. Joe
17. Nick
18. Kevin
19. Nick
20. Kevin
21. Nick
22. Joe
23. Joe
24. Kevin
25. Nick

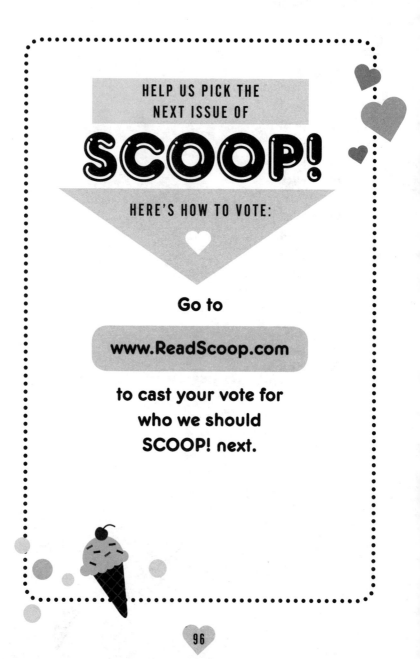

HELP US PICK THE
NEXT ISSUE OF

SCOOP!

HERE'S HOW TO VOTE:

Go to

www.ReadScoop.com

to cast your vote for
who we should
SCOOP! next.